HANDEL
THE FIRST BOOK FOR PIANISTS

EDITED BY GEROGE LUCKTENBERG

MW00559106

CONTENTS

ABOUT THE COMPOSER

1685 was a memorable year for music and in particular, for keyboard music. On February 23rd, in Halle, Germany, George Frideric Handel was born. The same year witnessed the birth of Johann Sebastian Bach and Domenico Scarlatti. Though the careers of these giants of the late Baroque style ran in strikingly different directions, they shared one distinction in common: all three were among the greatest keyboard performers, improvisers, and composers of their own and of all time.

Handel's father was an elderly barber-surgeon who intended a legal career for George. How the boy acquired an early proficiancy at the keyboard is unknown, but at the age of eight his unusual talent came to the attention of the reigning Duke, who impressed upon the father the need for formal instruction. The young Handel was then given a thorough training of both the harpsichord and the organ. By age 11, he was already serving as a substitue organist for his teacher at church services. Among his earliest compositions were many small keyboard pieces and suites, some of which appeared later in reworked versions.

Handel's adult career was devoted mainly to large vocal works such as operas and oratorios. The *Messiah* is probably the best known and most often performed sacred oratorio ever written. However, he also found time to write some very attractive teaching pieces for his students, a few of which have been selected by this editor. In this book, realizations for the ornaments are provided in a simple form. Tempo indications are merely suggestions for a final or "recital" speed; less advanced pupils can play them with good effect at slower tempos. Similarly, dynamics, articulations, and phrase marks are only guidlines and may be altered to suit the taste of the teacher or student.

Second Edition
Copyright © MMV by Alfred Publishing Co., Inc.
All rights reserved. Printed in USA.
ISBN 0-7390-3953-9

Cover art: Landscape with Roman Ruins, *1740*
   by Giovanni Antonio Canaletto (1697–1768)
   Accademia, Venice, Italy
   Cameraphoto/Art Resource, New York

PASSEPIED IN C MAJOR

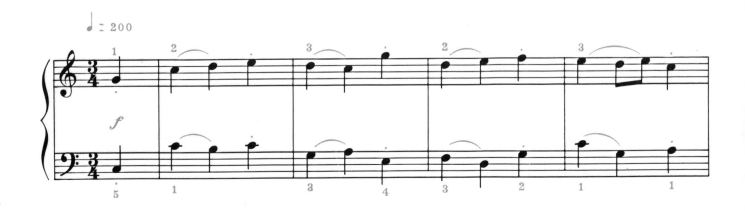

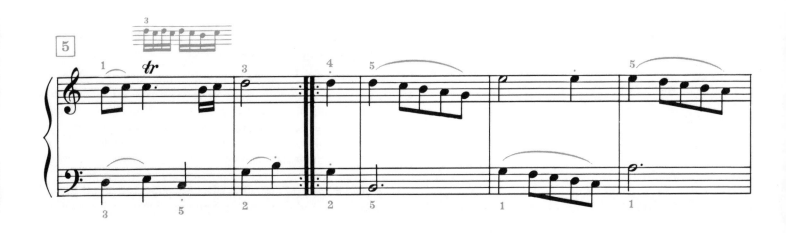

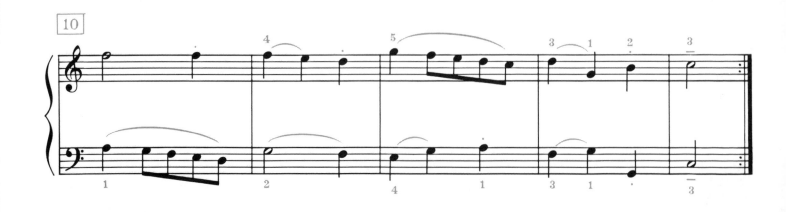

MENUET IN B MINOR

(a) The fermata (𝄐) indicates that the piece ends with that note after the repeat.

PASSEPIED IN A MAJOR

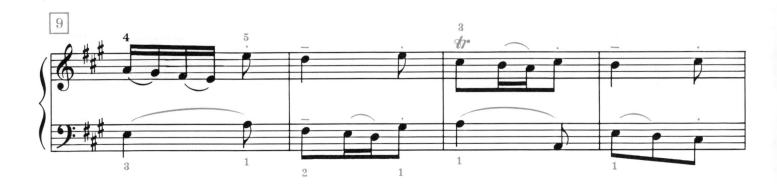

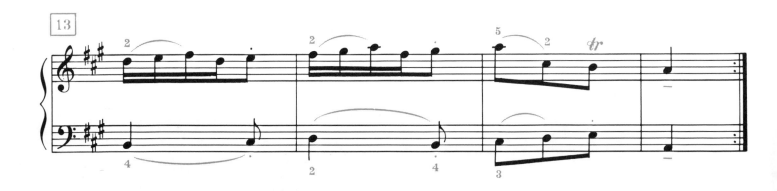

MENUET IN D MINOR

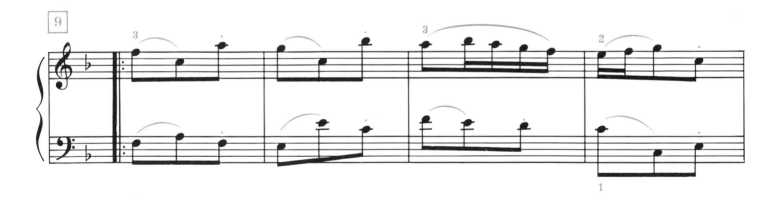

GAVOTTE IN G MAJOR

MENUET IN A MINOR

SUITE FOR A MUSICAL CLOCK

PRELUDE

The mechanical reproduction of music did not begin with Edison's phonograph. Large, elaborate music-boxes or organs operated by clockwork mechanisms were favorite playthings of the wealthy nobility. This miniature "sonata" appears in the "Aylesford" manuscripts. It also sounds well when played one octave higher than written, with plenty of pedal for a "music-box" effect.

ⓐ manuscript: G   ⓑ The double-stroke (♪) is an earlier form of trill-sign.

MENUET

10

AIR

GIGUE

IMPERTINENCE

(a) An extremely rare use of a programmatic title for Handel.

(b) or: [musical example]   (c) or: [musical example]

MENUET IN F MAJOR

AIR IN B FLAT MAJOR

(a) C?

SONATINA IN G MAJOR ⓐ

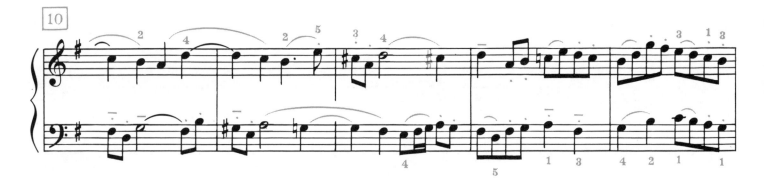

ⓐ Entitled "Fuga" in the "Aylesford" manuscript

ⓑ Manuscript: G

SONATINA B FLAT MAJOR

GAVOTTE IN G MINOR

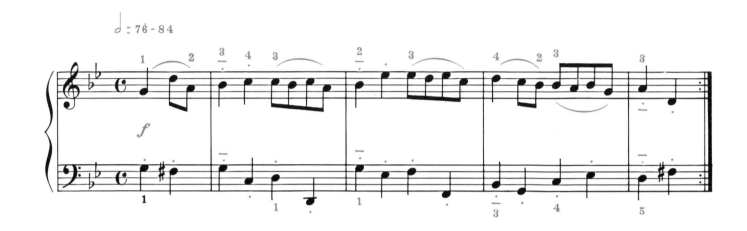

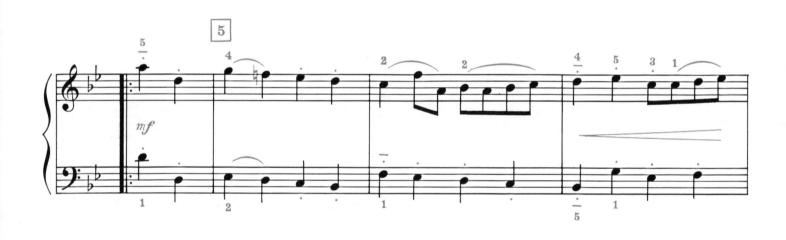

MENUET IN G MINOR

♩ = 120-132

(Da Capo)

mf

mp

Fine

(2nd time)

ⓐ

mf

f

Repeat; then Da Capo

ⓐ F?

TOCCATO

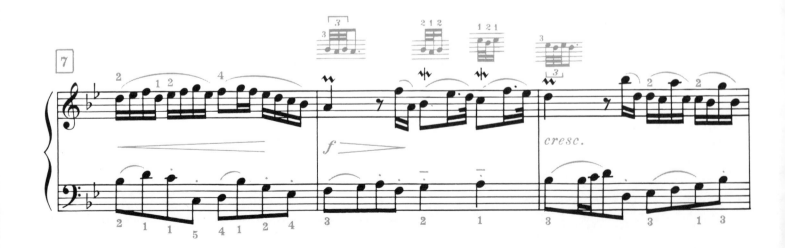

ENTRÉE

21

SARABAND IN D MINOR

JIGG IN D MINOR